KU-757-687

Important things that **must** be included

arie–Claude Dunleavy did the
rench stuff (with some help
from Alix Fontaine)

1 2 3 4 5 6 7 8 9   09 10 11 12

ISBN 978-0-07-161584-6
MHID 0-07-161584-9

McGraw-Hill books are available at special quantity discounts to use as premiums and sales promotions or for use in corporate training programs. To contact a representative, please visit the Contact Us pages at www.mhprofessional.com.

This book is printed on acid-free paper.
Printed and bound by Tien Wah Press, Singapore.

3

What's inside

Making friends

How to be cool with the group

Wanna play?

Our guide to joining in everything from hide-and-seek to the latest electronic game

Feeling hungry

Order your favorite foods or go local

Looking good

Make sure you keep up with all those essential fashions

Hanging out

At the pool, beach, or theme park—don't miss out on the action 70

Pocket money

Spend it here! 90

Grown-up talk

blah!
blah!
blah!
blah!

If you really, really have to! 100

Extra stuff

All the handy things—numbers, months, time, days of the week 108

my big brother
mon grand frère
mo gro frair
grandpa
papi
pah-pee
grandma
mamie
ma-mee
dad
papa
pah-pah
mom
maman
ma-mon
my little sister
ma petite sœur
ma pteet sir

Half a step this way

stepfather/stepmother
beau-père/belle-mère
👄 bow pair/bel mair

stepbrother/stepsister
beau-frère/belle-sœur
👄 bow frair/bel sir

half brother/half sister
demi frère/demi sœur
👄 dumee frair/dumee sir

Hi! Salut!
👄 saloo

What's your name?
Comment tu t'appelles?
👄 ko-mo too tapel

My name's ...
Je m'appelle ...
👄 jer mapel

Kissing is extremely popular among French children. You can't possibly say hello to your friends in the morning without kissing them on both cheeks. Try this in front of your mirror if your friends at home won't let you experiment on them.

from Canada
du Canada
👄 doo kana-da

from Ireland
d'Irlande
👄 deer-lond

from Scotland
d'Écosse
👄 day-cos

from Wales
du Pays de Galles
👄 doo pay-ee duh gal

from the U.S.
des États-Unis
👄 days etaz-oo-nee

from England
d'Angleterre
👄 donglutair

10

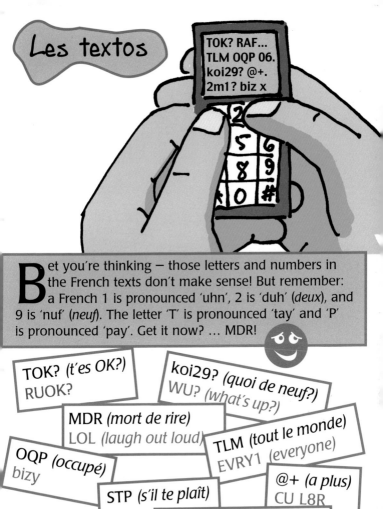

Les textos

Phone screen:
TOK? RAF...
TLM OQP 06.
koi29? @+.
2m1? biz x

Bet you're thinking – those letters and numbers in the French texts don't make sense! But remember: a French 1 is pronounced 'uhn', 2 is 'duh' (*deux*), and 9 is 'nuf' (*neuf*). The letter 'T' is pronounced 'tay' and 'P' is pronounced 'pay'. Get it now? ... MDR!

TOK? *(t'es OK?)*
RUOK?

koi29? *(quoi de neuf?)*
WU? *(what's up?)*

MDR *(mort de rire)*
LOL *(laugh out loud)*

TLM *(tout le monde)*
EVRY1 *(everyone)*

OQP *(occupé)*
bizy

@+ *(a plus)*
CU L8R

STP *(s'il te plaît)*
PLZ

RAF *(rien a faire)*
nufN2do *(nothing to do)*

2m1 *(demain)*
2moro

biz *(bisous)*
luv

06 *(aussi)*
2 *(too)*

11

How old are you?
T'as quel âge?
👄 ta kel azh

12 years old
Douze ans
👄 dooz on

Happy birthday!
Bon anniversaire!
👄 bon anee-versair

What's your star sign?
C'est quoi, ton signe astrologique?
👄 say kwa toh seen-yastrolojeek

When's your birthday?
C'est quand, ton anniversaire?
👄 say kon, ton anee-versair

Star signs

AQUARIUS
Jan. 21 – Feb. 19
le Verseau 😚 lerver-so

PISCES
Feb. 20 – Mar. 20
les Poissons 😚 lay pwason

ARIES
Mar. 21 – Apr. 20
le Bélier 😚 ler belly-er

TAURUS
Apr. 21 – May 21
le Taureau 😚 ler tor-oh

GEMINI
May 22 – June 21
les Gémeaux 😚 lay jem-oh

CANCER
June 22 – July 23
le Cancer 😚 ler cancer

LEO
July 24 – Aug. 23
le Lion 😚 ler lee-on

VIRGO
Aug. 24 – Sep. 23
la Vierge 😚 la vee-erj

LIBRA
Sep. 24 – Oct. 23
la Balance 😚 la ba-lons

SCORPIO
Oct. 24 – Nov. 22
le Scorpion 😚 ler scorpion

SAGITTARIUS
Nov. 23 – Dec. 21
le Sagittaire 😚 ler sajitair

CAPRICORN
Dec. 22 – Jan. 20
le Capricorne 😚 ler capricorn

13

soccer **le foot**
👄 ler foot

rollerblading **le roller**
👄 ler roller

music **la musique**
👄 la mew-zeek

electronic games **les jeux électroniques**
👄 lay jer ay-lek-tro-neek

tv **la télé**
👄 la taylay

comics **la BD**
👄 la bay-day

teddy bears **les nounours**
👄 lay noonoor

school **l'école**
👄 lay-kol

spiders **les araignées**
👄 layz aran-nyay

15

What's your favorite ...?

Quel est ton/ta ... préféré(e)?

👄 kel ay ton/tah ... preh-fairay

group
(ton) groupe
👄 (ton) groop

color
(ta) couleur
👄 (tah) koo-ler

→ Page 69

game
(ton) jeu
👄 (ton) jer

snack
(ton) goûter
👄 (ton) gootay

ring tone
(ta) sonnerie
👄 (tah) soneree

animal
(ton) animal
👄 (ton) a-nee-mal

team
(ton) équipe
👄 (ton) ekeep

17

Talk about your pets

He's hungry
Il a faim
👄 eel ah fam

She's sleeping
Elle fait dodo 👄 el fay dodo

Can I pet your dog?
Je peux caresser ton chien
👄 jer per karessay ton shyan

Do you have any pets?
T'as des animaux de compagnie?
👄 tah dayz ani-moh duh kopanye

dog
le chien
👄 ler shee–an

cat
le chat
👄 ler sha

snake
le serpent
👄 ler sir–pon

guinea pig
le cochon d'Inde
👄 ler ko–shon d'and

hamster
le hamster
👄 ler amster

parakeet
la perruche
👄 la peroosh

My little doggy goes *oua-oua-oua!*

A French doggy (that's "toutou" in baby language) doesn't say "woof, woof," it says *"oua, oua"* (*waa-waa*). A French sheep says *"bêê, bêê!"* (*bear-bear*) and a cluck-cluck in French chicken-speak is *"cot-cot"* (*ko-ko*). But cats do say "miaow" whether they're speaking French or English!

19

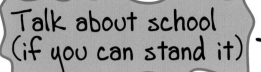

Talk about school (if you can stand it)

geography
la géo
👄 la jay-o

PE
la gym
👄 la jeem

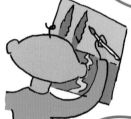

art
le dessin
👄 ler dessa

French
le français
👄 ler fron-say

math
les maths
👄 lay mat

20

English
l'anglais
👄 lon-glay

music
la musique
👄 la mew-zeek

English
m. smith
i love sandra
x x x

history
l'histoire
👄 lis-twar

science
les sciences
👄 lay see-yons

21

IT
l'informatique
👄 lanfor-mateek

Way unfair!

French children have very long vacation breaks: 9 weeks in the summer and another 6–7 weeks throughout the rest of the year. But before you turn green with envy, you might not like the mounds of "**devoirs de vacances**" (*duh-vwa duh vacans*), that's "vacation homework!" And if you fail your exams, the teachers could make you repeat the whole year with your little sister!

Talk about your phone

That's ancient
Il est super vieux!
👄 eel ay super vyuh

I've run out of credit
J'ai plus de forfait
👄 jay ploo duh forfay

What's your phone like?
Il est comment ton portable?
👄 eel ay komon ton portabler

Lucky!
Trop de chance!
👄 troh duh shons

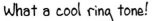

What a cool ring tone!
Elle est géniale ta sonnerie!
👄 el ay jenyal ta soneree

Gossip

Can you keep a secret?
Tu peux garder un secret?
👄 too per garday er sekray

Do you have a boyfriend (a girlfriend)?
T'as un petit ami (une petite amie)?
👄 tah er pteet amee (oon pteet amee)

An OK guy/An OK girl
Un mec sympa/Une fille sympa
👄 er mek sampa/oon fee sampa

Way bossy!
Quel commandant!
👄 kel comon-don

He/She's nutty!
Il/Elle est dingue!
👄 eel/el ay dang

What a creep!
Quel râleur!
👄 kel rah-ler

24

You won't make many friends saying this!

Shut up!
La ferme!
👄 la ferm

Bug off!
Dégage!
👄 Day-gaj

If you're fed up with someone, and you want to say something like "you silly …!" or "you stupid …!", you can start with ***"espèce de"*** (which actually means "piece of …") and add anything you like. What about …

Stupid banana!
Espèce de banane!
(espes duh banan)

or …

Silly sausage!
Espèce d'andouille!
(espes don-dooy)

Take your pick. It should do the trick. You could also try ***"espèce d'idiot!"*** *(espes dee-dyo)*. You don't need a translation here, do you?

25

Fudge!
La vache!
👄 la vash

Rats!
Zut!
👄 zoot

"Did someone call me?"

← la vache

That's not funny
C'est pas marrant
👄 say pah marror

That's plenty!
C'est bon!
👄 say bon

I'm fed up
J'en ai ras-le-bol
👄 jon nay ral-bol

Stop!
Arrête!
👄 aret

I want to go home!
Je veux rentrer chez moi
👄 jer ver rentray
shay mwah

I don't care
Je m'en fiche
👄 jer mon feesh

At last!
C'est pas trop tôt!
👄 say pah tro toe

27

Saying good-bye

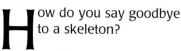

What's your address?
Tu m'donnes ton adresse?
👄 too mdon ton adres

Here's my address
Voilà mon adresse
👄 vla mon adres

Come to visit me
Viens chez moi
👄 vya shay mwa

H ow do you say goodbye to a skeleton?

Bone Voyage!

Have a good trip!
Bon voyage!
👄 bon vwoy-arj

Write to me soon
Écris-moi vite
👄 ekree mwa veet

Send me a text
Envois-moi un texto
👄 onvwa-mwa er texto

Let's chat on-line
On chat sur internet
👄 on "chat" syur internet

Bye!
Au revoir!
👄 oh rev-wa

What's your email?
C'est quoi ton e-mail?
👄 say kwa ton e-mail

ꀭ☐@ℨ◇*@ᴙ.com

WANNA PLAY?

l'élastique
👄 lelasteek

le ping-pong
👄 ler "ping pong"

le baladeur
👄 ler balad-er

le yo-yo
👄 ler yo-yo

le portable
👄 ler porta-bler

WANNA PLAY?

Do you want to play ...?
Tu veux jouer ...?
👄 too ver joo-ay

... foos-ball?
... au baby-foot?
👄 oh baby foot

... cards?
... aux cartes?
👄 oh kart

... on the computer?
... sur l'ordinateur?
👄 syur lordee-nater

... tic-tac-toe?
... au morpion?
👄 oh more-pyon

... hide and seek?
... à cache-cache?
👄 a kash kash

... catch?
... au ballon?
👄 oh ballo

Not now.
Pas maintenant
👄 pah mat-non

Yeah!
Ouais!
👄 oo-way

33

Care for a game of **cat** or **leap sheep**?!

In France, playing tag is called playing "at cat"—**à chat** (*asha*). Whoever is "it" is the cat—**le chat** (*ler sha*). And you don't play "leap frog," you play "leap sheep"—**saute mouton** (*sote moo-ton*). Have you ever seen a sheep leaping? I ask you!

Can my friend play too?
Mon copain peut jouer aussi?
✆ mo kopan per jooway oh-see

I have to ask my parents
Il faut que je demande à mes vieu
✆ eel foh ker jer daymon ah may vyu

Who dares?

You're it!
Touché!
👄 tooshay

Race you!
On fait la course?
👄 on fay la koors?

I'm first
C'est moi le premier
👄 say mwa ler pre-myay

36

37

Electronic games

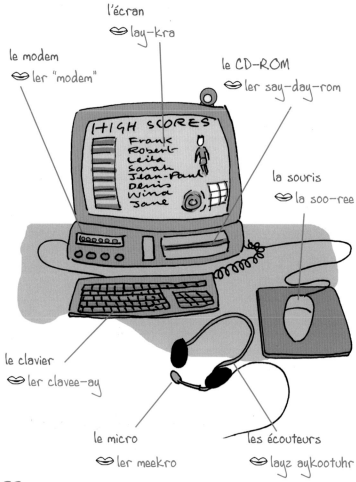

l'écran
☞ lay-kra

le modem
☞ ler "modem"

le CD-ROM
☞ ler say-day-rom

la souris
☞ la soo-ree

le clavier
☞ ler clavee-ay

le micro
☞ ler meekro

les écouteurs
☞ layz aykootuhr

Show me
Montre-moi
 montrer mwa

What do I do?
Qu'est-ce que je fais?
 kesker jer fay

Am I dead?
Ch'suis mort?
 shwee more

Shoot-em-up!
Tue-les!
 tew-lay

How many lives do I have?
J'ai combien de vies?
 jay konbee-yah duh vee

How many levels are there?
Y'a combien de niveaux?
 yah konbee-yah de neevo

It's virtual fun!

Do you have a webcam?
T'as une webcam?
👄 ta oon "webcam"

send me a message
envois-moi un message

how do i join?
comment je m'inscris?

i'm not old enough
je suis pas assez grand

i'm not allowed
j'ai pas le droit

i don't know who you are
je sais pas qui vous êtes

my blog
mon blog
👄 mo "blog"

my contacts
mes contacts
👄 may kontakt

my photos
mes photos
👄 may foto

my videos
mes vidéos
👄 may vidayoh

my music ma musique
👄 ma mooseek

41

Non couch-potato activities!

tennis
le tennis
👄 ler "tennis"

trampolining
le trampoline
👄 ler "trampoline"

bowling
le bowling
👄 ler "bowling"

swimming
la natation
👄 la natasee-on

42

hockey
le hockey
👄 ler okee

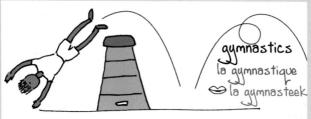

gymnastics
la gymnastique
👄 la gymnasteek

ballet
le ballet
👄 ler ballay

basketball   le basket
👄 ler basket

and, of course, we haven't forgotten *"le foot"* ...

43

soccer

cleats
les godasses
👄 lay godas

soccer gear
les affaires de foot
👄 layz afayr duh foot

ref
l'arbitre
👄 lar-beetrer

shin pads
les protèges-tibias
👄 lay protej-tibya

Well played!
Bien joué
👄 beeyah joo-way

Pass! Passe!
👄 pas

44

defender
le défenseur
👄 ler dayfon-sir

attacker
l'attaquant
👄 latakon

Foul!
Coup-franc!
👄 koo fron

He pushed me!
Il m'a poussé!
👄 eel ma poo-say

Penalty!
Le penalty!
👄 ler paynalty

Goal!
But!
👄 boot

46

Not like that!
Pas comme ça!
👄 pah kom sa

You cheat! Tricheur! (boys only)
Tricheuse! (girls only)
👄 tree-sher/tree-sherz

I'm not playing anymore
Je joue plus
👄 jer joo ploo

It's not fair!
C'est pas juste!
👄 say pah joost

Stop it!
Arrête!
👄 aret

47

Showing off

a handstand?
le poirier?
👄 ler pwa-riyay

Can you do ...
Tu sais faire ...
👄 too say fair

Look at me!
Regarde-moi!
👄 re-gard mwa

a cartwheel?
la roue?
👄 la roo

this?
ça?
👄 sa

Tongue tied

Impress your French friends with this!

You can show off to your new French friends by practising this tongue twister:

Si ces six sausissons-ci sont six sous, ces six sausissons-ci sont très chers

see say see soseeson see son see soo, say see soseeson see son tray shair

(This means "If these six sausages cost six sous, these six sausages are very expensive.")

Then see if they can do as well with this English one:

"She sells seashells on the seashore, but the shells she sells aren't seashells, I'm sure."

For a rainy day

deck of cards
un jeu de cartes
👄 er jer duh kart

my deal/your deal
à moi la donne/à toi la donne
👄 a mwa la don/a twa la don

king
le roi
👄 ler rwa

queen
la dame
👄 la dam

jack
le valet
👄 ler valay

joker
le joker
👄 ler jokair

trèfle
👄 tray-fler

cœur
👄 kur

pique
👄 peek

carreau
👄 karo

FEELING HUNGRY

hamburger
le steak haché
ler stek ashay

fries
les frites
lay freet

ice cream
la glace
la glas

coke
le coca
ler koka

snails
les escargots
👄 layz eskargo

mussels
les moules
👄 lay mool

caramel custard
la crème caramel
👄 la krem karamel

orange juice
le jus d'orange
👄 ler joo doronj

FEELING HUNGRY

Grub (la bouffe)

I'm starving
J'ai une faim de loup
👄 jay oon fam der loo

That means "I have the hunger of a wolf!"

le loup

Please can I have ...
Donnez-moi, s'il vous plaît ...
👄 donay mwa,
   seel voo play

... a chocolate pastry

un pain au chocolat

👄 er pan oh shokolah

... a croissant

un croissant

👄 er kruh-son

... an apple turnover

un chausson aux pommes

👄 er show-son oh pom

... a chocolate eclair

un éclair au chocolat

👄 er eklair oh shokolah

... a bun with raisins

un pain aux raisins

👄 er pan oh rayzan

Chocolate eclair? **"Miam, miam!"**
Snail pancake? **"Beurk!"**
If you're going to make food
noises, you'll need to know how
to do it properly in French!

"Yum, yum!" is out in French. You should
say **"Miam, miam!"** And "Yuk!" is
"Beurk" (pronounced "burk"), but
be careful not to let adults hear
you say this!

55

... a baguette
une baguette
👄 oon baget

... a pancake
une crêpe
👄 oon krep

... a waffle
une gaufre
👄 oon go-frer

Did you know?

A lot of children have hot chocolate for breakfast in the morning and some of them will dip their bread or croissants in it. It gets very soggy and Mom is sure not to like this!

I'm dying for a drink

Je meurs
de soif
👄 jer mur
der swaf

I'd like ...
Je voudrais ...
👄 jer voodray

... a coke
... un coca
👄 er koka

... an orange juice
... un jus d'orange
👄 er joo doronj

... an apple juice
... un jus de pommes
👄 er joo der pom

57

... a lemon soda

... une limonade
👄 oon leemonad

You can also have your lemon soda with flavored syrup—then it's called a "***diabolo***." The most well-known is "***diabolo menthe***", lemonade with mint syrup—hmmm!

... a syrup
un sirop
👄 er seero

... a milkshake
... un milkshake
👄 er meelkshek

You get your hot chocolate in a bowl (and that, at least, is a decent amount).

... a hot chocolate
... un chocolat
👄 er shokolah

How did you like it?

That's lovely
C'est super-bon
😋 say soopair-bon

That's yummy
C'est géant
😋 say jay-on

I don't like that
J'aime pas ça
😋 jem pah sa

I'm stuffed
J'ai trop bouffé
😋 jay tro boofay

I can't eat that
Je mange pas ça
😋 jer monj pah sa

That's gross
C'est dégoûtant
😋 say day-gooton

59

A "crunchy man" sandwich, please.

You never thought you could crunch up a man in France and get away with it, did you? Well, in France a grilled ham-and-cheese sandwich is:

un croque-monsieur
👄 er krok murs-yur

… that means a "crunchy man." There's also a "crunchy woman!"

un croque-madame
👄 er krok ma-dam

… which is the same but with a fried egg on top.

Tales of snails

Did you know that snails have to be put in a bucket of salt water for three days to clean out their insides (don't ask!). After that they are baked in the oven in their shells and eaten with tons of garlic butter. And many French kids still love them!

Parties

French children often sing "Happy Birthday" in English when the candles are blown out on the cake. So you can practice singing the words with a French accent!

balloon la balle
👄 la bal

appee birzday too yoo!
appee birzday too yoo!

Can I have some more?
Je peux en avoir d'autre?
👄 jer per on avwah door-truh

party hat
le chapeau cotillon
👄 ler shapoh koteeyon

This is for you
C'est pour toi
👄 say poor twa

61

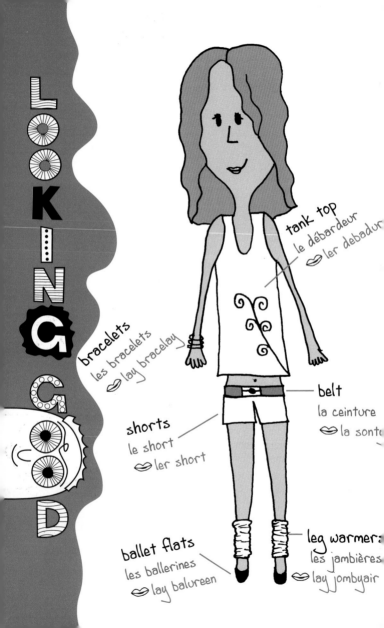

LOOKING GOOD

tank top
le débardeur
👄 ler debadur

bracelets
les bracelets
👄 lay bracelay

belt
la ceinture
👄 la sonto

shorts
le short
👄 ler short

leg warmers
les jambières
👄 lay jombyair

ballet flats
les ballerines
👄 lay balureen

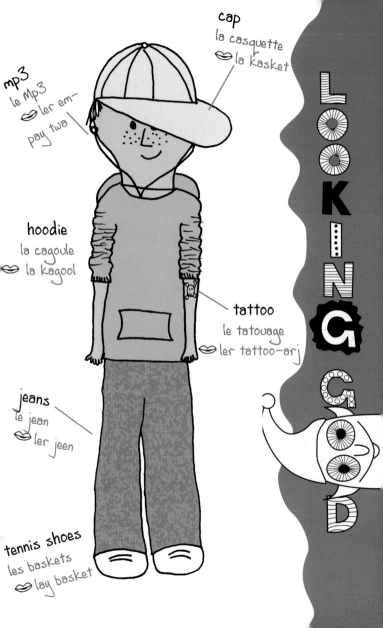

cap
la casquette
🗣 la kasket

mp3
le Mp3
🗣 ler em-
pay twa

hoodie
la cagoule
🗣 la kagool

tattoo
le tatouage
🗣 ler tattoo-arj

jeans
le jean
🗣 ler jeen

tennis shoes
les baskets
🗣 lay basket

LOOKING GOOD

spotted
à pois
👄 a pwa

flowery à fleurs
👄 a fler

frilly
à frous-frous
👄 a froo froo

glittery
à paillettes
👄 a pie-et

striped à rayures
👄 a rayure

65

Clothes

sweatshirt
le sweat
👄 ler swe

jeans
le jean
👄 ler "jean"

T-shirt
le T-shirt
👄 ler "T-shirt"

soccer shirt
le maillot de foot
👄 ler mayo der foot

tennis shoes
les baskets
👄 lay basket

shoes
les chaussures
👄 lay show-soor

66

skirt
la jupe
👄 la joop

dress
la robe
👄 la rob

pants
le pantalon
👄 ler panta-lon

Where's my pant?!

The French don't wear "pant**s**" or "jean**s**," they wear only one of them: un pantalon *(er pantaloh)*; un jean *(er jeen)*. Strange, could've sworn they had two legs!

67

Make it up!

lip gloss
le gloss
ler gloss

glitter gel
le gel à paillettes
ler jel a pie-yet

nail polish
le vernis à ongles
ler vairnee a ongluh

earrings
les boucles d'oreilles
lay boo-kluh doray

I need a mirror
J'ai besoin d'un miroir
jay buzwa dun mirwa

eye shadow
le fard à paupières
ler fardah po-pyair

Can you lend
me your
flat iron?
Tu peux me prêter
ton fer à lisser?
too per mer
pretay ton fair a
leezay

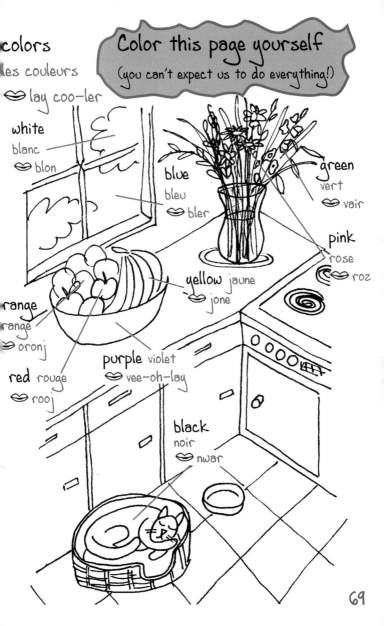

colors

les couleurs
👄 lay coo-ler

Color this page yourself
(you can't expect us to do everything!)

white
blanc
👄 blon

blue
bleu
👄 bler

green
vert
👄 vair

pink
rose
👄 roz

yellow jaune
👄 jone

orange
orange
👄 oronj

purple violet
👄 vee-oh-lay

red rouge
👄 rooj

black
noir
👄 nwar

69

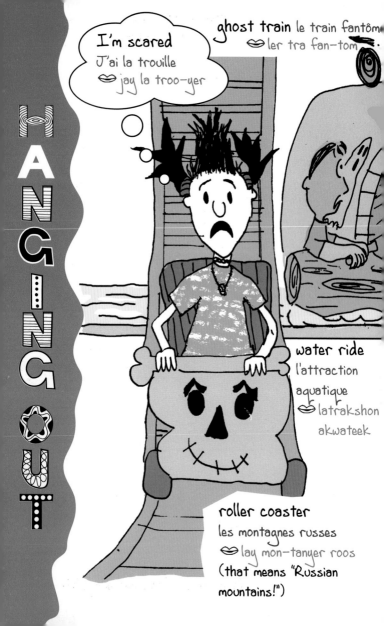

What should we do?
Qu'est-ce qu'on fait?
👄 kesk on fay

Can I come?
Je peux venir?
👄 jer per vuneer

Where do you all hang out?
Où trainez-vous?
👄 oo trainay voo

That's mega!
C'est géant!
👄 say jay-on

I'm (not) allowed
J'ai (pas) le droit
👄 jay (pa) ler drwa

Let's go back On y retourne
☞ onny rutoorn

That gives me goose bumps (or "chicken flesh" in French!)
Ça m'donne la chair de poule
☞ sa mdon la shair der pool

I'm scared
J'ai la trouille
☞ jay la troo-yer

I'm bored to death
C'est mortel
☞ say mortell

HOUSE OF MIRRORS

That's funny
C'est marrant
☞ say maron

73

Beach babes

Can I borrow this?
Tu me prêtes ça?
🗣 too mer pret sa

Let's hit the beac[h]
On va à la plage
🗣 on va a la plarj

Is this your bucket?
C'est ton seau?
🗣 say toh so

You can bury me
Tu peux m'enterrer
🗣 too per moterray

Stop throwing sand!
Arrête de jeter du sable!
🗣 arret der jetay dew sabler

Watch out for my eyes!
Attention à mes yeux!
🗣 attensee-on
a maiz yer

74

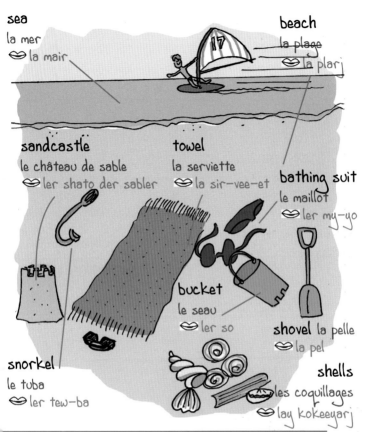

sea
la mer
👄 la mair

beach
la plage
👄 la plarj

sandcastle
le château de sable
👄 ler shato der sabler

towel
la serviette
👄 la sir-vee-et

bathing suit
le maillot
👄 ler my-yo

bucket
le seau
👄 ler so

shovel la pelle
👄 la pel

snorkel
le tuba
👄 ler tew-ba

shells
les coquillages
👄 lay kokeeyarj

How to get rid of your parents and eat lots of chocolate!

In France there are great beach clubs that organize all sorts of games as well as competitions (sandcastles, sports, etc.). The prizes are often given by large companies who make kids' stuff such as chocolate and toys. Insist on signing up!

75

It's going swimmingly!

How to make a splash in French!

PLOUF

Let's hit the swimming pool
On va à la piscine
👄 on va a la piseen

Can you swim (underwater
Tu sais nager (sous l'eau)?
👄 too say najay (soo lo)

Me too/I can't
Moi aussi/Moi pas
👄 mwa os-see/ mwa pa

Can you dive?
Tu sais plonger?
👄 too say plonjay

I'm getting changed
Je me change 👄 jer mer shanj

Can you do ...?
Tu sais faire ...?
👄 too say fair

backstroke
le dos crawlé
👄 ler doe krolay

butterfly
le papillon
👄 ler papeeyon

crawl
le crawl
👄 ler krol

breaststroke
la brasse 👄 la brass

slide
le tobogan
👄 ler tobogan

goggles
les lunettes de plongée
👄 lay loonet
der plonjay

77

Downtown

Do you know the way?
Tu connais le chemin?
👄 too konay ler shema

Let's ask
On va demander
👄 o va demonday

bus
le bus
👄 ler boos

Pooper-scoopers on wheels!

You might see bright green-and-white motorcycles with funny vacuum cleaners on the side riding around town scooping up the dog poop. The people riding the bikes look like astronauts! (Well, you'd want protection too, wouldn't you?)

Is it far?
C'est loin?
👄 say lwan

Are we allowed in here?
On a le droit d'entrer ici?
👄 on a ler drwa dentray eessee

car la bagnole
👄 la banyol

The "proper" French word for car is **"voiture"** (*vwat-yure*), but you'll look very uncool saying this. Stick to **"bagnole"** (*banyol*), or if the car is a wreck, try **"tacot"** (*taco*) for even more street cred: **"Quel tacot!"** (*kel tako*—"What an old clunker!").

Park yourself here

swings la balançoire
👄 la balonswar

jungle gym la cage à pou[u]
👄 la kaj ah pool

playground l'aire de jeu
👄 lair der jer

grass l'herbe
👄 lairb

tree l'arbre
👄 larbruh

slide
le toboggan
👄 ler tobogan

park le parc 👄 ler park

Can we play ball games?
On peut jouer au ballon?
👄 on per jooway oh balon

merry-go-round
le tourniquet
👄 ler toornikay

sandbox
le bac à sable
👄 ler bakah sabluh

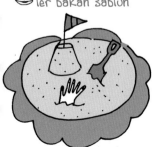

Can I have a go? Je peux
essayer? 👄 jer per esay-yay

81

Picnic (le pique-nique)

I hate wasps
Je déteste les guêpes
👄 jer daytest
lay gep

Move over!
Pousse-toi!
👄 poos twa

bread
le pain 👄 ler pan

Let's sit here
On s'assoie ici?
👄 on saswa eessee

napkin
la serviette
👄 la sir-vee-et

ham le jambon
👄 ler jambon

cheese
le fromage
👄 ler fromarj

yogurt
le yaourt
👄 ler ya-oort

chips
les chips
👄 lay sheep

drinks
les boissons
👄 lay bwason

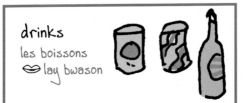

knife
le couteau
👄 ler koo-toe

spoon
la cuillère
👄 la kwee-yeah

fork
la fourchette
👄 la four-shet

wasps
les guêpes
👄 lay gep

bees
les abeilles
👄 layz abay

bzzzz

ants
les fourmis
👄 lay foor-mee

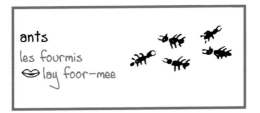

Wake up, campers!

tent la tente
👄 la tont

tent peg
le piquet de tente
👄 ler peekay der ton

camper van
le camping-car
👄 ler komping car

pen knife
le couteau suisse
👄 ler kootoh swees

camping stove
le camping gaz
👄 ler komping gaz

sleeping bag le sac de couchage
👄 ler sak der kooshaj

flashlight
la lampe de poche
👄 la lomp
der posh

84

That tent's a palace!
Cette tente, c'est la classe!
👄 set tont, say la klas

campfire
le feu de camp
👄 ler fer der komp

I've lost my flashlight
J'ai paumé ma lampe de poche
👄 jay pomay ma lomp der posh

These showers are gross
Ces douches sont crades
👄 say doosh son krad

Where does the garbage go?
Où est-ce qu'on jette les ordures?
👄 oo eskon jet layz ordyur

All the fun of the fair

slide
le toboggan
👄 ler tobogan

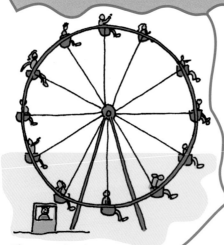

Ferris wheel
la grande roue
👄 la grond roo

house of mirrors
le palais des glaces
👄 ler palay day glas

bumper cars
les autos tamponneuses
👄 layz oto tomponerz

Let's try this
On essaie ça?
👄 on essay sa

Disco nights

mirror ball
la boule multi-facettes
👄 la bool multee-faset

loudspeakers
les enceintes
👄 layz onsent

Can I request a song?
Je peux demander qu'on passe une chanson? 👄 jer per dumonday kon pas oon shonso

The music is really lame
La musique est vraiment nulle
👄 la mooseek ay vraymon nool

spotlights
les spots
👄 lay spot

DJ le DJ
👄 ler "DJ"

mixing desk la table de mixage 👄 la table der meeksarj

How old do I need to be?

Quel âge il faut avoir?

👄 kel aj eel foh avwah

dance floor

la piste de danse

👄 la peest der dons

Let's dance!

On danse!

👄 on dons

I love this song!

J'adore cette chanson!

👄 jadoor set shonso

89

POCKET MONEY

candy
les bonbons
👄 lay bonbon

les T-shirts
👄 lay "T-shirt"

toys les jouets
👄 lay joo-ay

le vendeur
👄 ler von-du

books
les livres
👄 lay lee-vrer

le mobile
👄 ler mobeel

les crayons
👄 lay crayon
Watch out! This means *pencils* NOT crayons!

What does that sign say?

pâtisserie
cake shop
👄 pateesree

boucherie
butcher shop
👄 booshree

boulangerie
bakery
👄 boolonjree

confiserie
candy store
👄 konfeesree

papeterie
office supplies
👄 paptree

épicerie
grocery store
👄 aypeesree

boutique de vêtements
clothes shop
👄 booteek der vetmon

92

Do you have some cash?
T'as des sous?
👄 tah day soo

I'm broke
Je suis fauché
👄 jer swee foshay

I'm loaded
J'ai plein d'sous
👄 jay pla dsoo

Here you go
Voilà
👄 vla

That's a weird shop!
Quel magasin bizarre!
👄 kel maguzah beezar

That's a bargain C'est pas cher
👄 say pa shair

It's a rip-off
C'est du vol
👄 say dew vol

93

Sweet heaven!

I love this shop
J'adore cette boutique
👄 jadore set booteek

Let's get some candy
On va acheter des bonbons
👄 on va ashtay day bonbon

Let's get some ice cream
On va acheter une glace
👄 on va ashtay oon glas

lollipops
des sucettes
👄 day sooset

a bar of chocolate
une tablette de chocolat
👄 oon tablet der shokola

chewing gum
chewing gum
👄 just say it, will you!

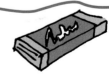

If you really want to look French and end up with lots of fillings, ask for:

des Carambars™ (day caram–bar)

medium-hard toffee-bars, also available in all sorts of fruity flavors; popular for the desperately silly jokes to be found inside the wrappings

des Malabars™ (day malabar)

bubble-gum, also popular for the tattoos provided with them

des nounours en chocolat (day noonoors on shokola)

teddy-shaped marshmallow-type candy in chocolate coating

des frites (day freet)

fruity gums, slightly fizzy, shaped like fries

des Mini Berlingot™ (day mini berlingo)

sugary creamy stuff sold in small squishy packets — a bit like a small version of the "lunchbox" yogurts

des Dragibus™ (day drajibus)

multicolored licorice jelly beans

95

Other things you could buy

(that won't ruin your teeth!)

What are you getting?
Qu'est-ce tu prends?
👄 keska too pron

That toy, please
Ce jouet là, s'il vous plaît
👄 ser joo-ay la, seel voo pla

Two postcards, please
Deux cartes postales,
s'il vous plaît
👄 der kart
post-tal,
seel voo play

This is garbage
C'est nul
👄 say nool

This is cool
C'est cool
👄 say kool

I'm getting ...

J'achète ... 👄 jashait

... a pen un stylo
👄 er stee-lo

... stamps
des timbres
👄 day timbrer

... felt-tip pens
des feutres
👄 day fer-trer

... colored pencils
des crayons de couleur
👄 day krayon der koolur

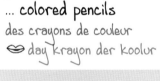

... a key ring
un porte-clés
👄 er port klay

... comics
des BD
👄 day bay day

... a fridge magnet

un aimant

👄 er aymon

... a shell box

une boîte à coquillages

👄 oon bwat ah kokeeyaj

... a CD

un CD

👄 er say-day

How much is that?

C'est combien?

👄 say kombee-yah

For many years France's favorite comics have been Astérix and Tintin. They have both been translated into English, as well as into many other languages. Today children also like to read:

Tom Tom et Nana
Boule et Bill
Natacha
Gaston Lagaffe

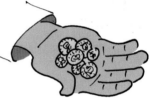

Money talks

How much pocket money do you get?

T'as combien d'argent de poche?
👄 tah komee-yah darjon der posh

I only have this much

J'ai seulement ça
👄 jay sulmo sah

No way!

Pas question!
👄 pa kes-tyo

Can you lend me ten euros?

Tu peux me prêter dix euros
👄 too per mer pretay dee yooro

Money talk

French money is the **euro** (pronounced *ew-roh*).
A euro is divided into 100 **centimes** (*senteem*).
Coins: 1, 2, 5, 10, 20, 50 **centimes**

   1, 2 **euros**

Notes: 5, 10, 20, 50, 100 **euros**

Make sure you know how much you are spending before you blow all your pocket money at once!

Something has dropped/broken
Quelque chose est tombé/cassé
👄 kel-ker shose ay tombay/kassay

Please
S'il vous plaît
👄 seel voo play

Can you help me?
Vous pouvez m'aider?
👄 voo poovay mayday

Where's the mailbox?
Où est la boîte aux lettres?
👄 oo ay la bwat oh lettrer

Where are the toilets?
Où sont les toilettes?
👄 oo son lay twalet

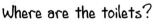

102

I can't manage it
Je n'y arrive pas
👄 jer nee arreev pah

Could you pass me that?
Vous pouvez me passer ça?
👄 voo poovay mer passay sa

What time is it?
Quelle heure il est?
👄 kel ur eelay

Come and see
Venez voir
👄 venay vwar

May I look at your watch?
Je peux voir sur votre montre?
👄 jer per vwar syur votrer montrer

103

Lost for words

... **my ticket**
mon billet
👄 mo beeyay

I've lost ...
J'ai perdu ...
👄 jay perdew

... **my parents**
mes parents
👄 may paron

... **my phone**
mon portable
👄 mo
portabluh

... **my shoes**
mes chaussures
👄 may sho-syur

... **my money** mon argent
👄 mo arjon

... **my sweater**
mon pull
👄 mo pool

... **my watch**
ma montre
👄 ma montrer

... **my jacket** ma veste
👄 ma vest

ADULTS ONLY!

Show this page to adults who can't seem to make themselves clear (it happens). They will point to a phrase, you read what they mean, and you should all understand each other perfectly.

Ne t'en fais pas
Don't worry

Assieds-toi ici
Sit down here

Quel est ton nom et ton prénom?
What's your name and surname?

Quel âge as-tu?
How old are you?

D'où viens-tu?
Where are you from?

Où habites-tu?
Where are you staying?

Où est-ce que tu as mal?
Where does it hurt?

Est-ce que tu es allergique à quelque chose?
Are you allergic to anything?

C'est interdit
It's forbidden

Tu dois être accompagné d'un adulte
You have to have an adult with you

Je vais chercher quelqu'un qui parle anglais
I'll get someone who speaks English

EXTRA STUFF

weather
le temps
👄 ler toh

numbers les nombres
👄 lay nombruh

time

l'heure

lur

EXTRA STUFF

There was an English cat called "one, two, three" and a French cat called "un, deux, trois" standing waiting to cross a river. Both were afraid of water, so the English cat suggested that they race across to make it more fun. Who won?

Answer: "One, two, three" because "un, deux, trois" CAT SANK!

un   un

deux   der

trois   twa

quatre   katrer

cinq   sank

six   sees

110

sept ☺ set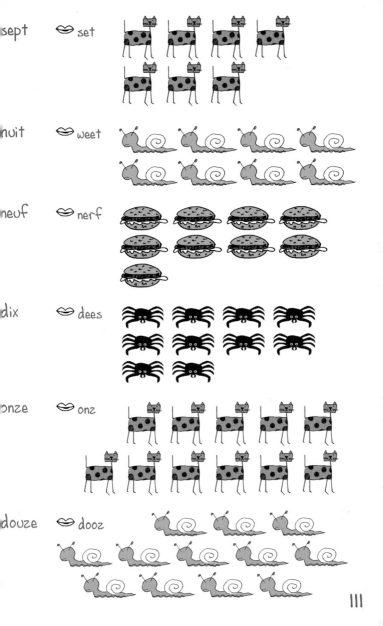

huit ☺ weet

neuf ☺ nerf

dix ☺ dees

onze ☺ onz

douze ☺ dooz

111

treize 👄 trez

quatorze 👄 catorz

quinze 👄 kanz

16 seize	*sez*	19 dix-neuf	*dees-nerf*
17 dix-sept	*dees-set*	20 vingt	*van*
18 dix-huit	*dees-weet*		

If you want to say "twenty-two," "sixty-five,"
and so on, you can just put the two numbers
together like you do in English:

22 **vingt-deux**   *van der*

65 **soixante cinq** *swasont sank*

This works except if you're saying "twenty-
one," "sixty-one," and so on. Then you need to
add the word for "and" (**et**) in the middle:

21 **vingt et un**   *vant eh un*

61 **soixante et un** *swasont eh un*

30 trente	*tront*
40 quarante	*karont*
50 cinquante	*sankont*
60 soixante	*swasont*
70 soixante-dix	*swasont dees*
80 quatre-vingts	*katrer van*
90 quatre-vingt-dix	*katrer van dees*
100 cent	*sonn*

The French must be really big on sums! Everything's fine until you reach 70. Instead of "seventy," they say "sixty-ten" (*soixante-dix*) and they keep counting like this until they reach 80. So 72 is "sixty-twelve" (*soixante douze*), 78 is "sixty-eighteen" (*soixante dix-huit*), and so on.

Just so it doesn't get too easy, for 80 they say "4 twenties!" And to really make your brain ache they continue like this until 100. So 90 is "4 twenties 10" (*quatre-vingt-dix*), 95 is "4 twenties fifteen" (*quatre-vingt-quinze*) … you did remember your calculator, didn't you??

1,000 mille *meel*

a million *un million* *uh meelyoh*

billions and billions! *des milliards de milliards!*
day meelyar der meelyar

March	mars	*mars*
April	avril	*avreel*
May	mai	*meh*

June	juin	*joo-wah*
July	juillet	*joowee-eh*
August	août	*oot*

September	septembre	*septombrer*
October	octobre	*octobrer*
November	novembre	*novombrer*

December	décembre	*desombrer*
January	janvier	*jonvee-eh*
February	février	*fevree-eh*

printemps   *prantom*

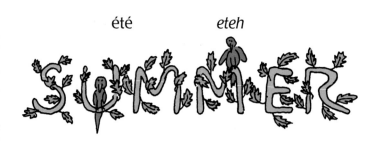

été   *eteh*

automne   *awtom*

hiver   *eever*

Monday	lundi	*lundee*
Tuesday	mardi	*mardee*
Wednesday	mercredi	*mecredee*
Thursday	jeudi	*jurdee*
Friday	vendredi	*vendrudee*
Saturday	samedi	*samdee*
Sunday	dimanche	*deemonsh*

By the way, French kids don't usually have school on Wednesdays, but they have to go on Saturday mornings. Still—that's half a day less than you!

Good times

It's ...
Il est ...
👄 eel ay

(one) o'clock
(une) heure
👄 (oon) ur

quarter after (two)
(deux heures) et quart
👄 (der zur) ay kar

quarter to (four)
(quatre heures) moins le quart
👄 (katr ur) mwan ler kar

half past (three)
(trois heures) et demie
👄 (twa zur) ay demee

five after (ten)

(dix heures) cinq

👄 dees ur sank

twenty after (eleven)

(onze heures) vingt

👄 onz ur van

ten to (four)

(quatre heures) moins dix

👄 (katr ur) mwan dees

twenty to (six)

(six heures) moins vingt

👄 (sees ur) mwan van

morning
matin
 ma-tah

midday
midi
 meedee

afternoon
après-midi
 apray meedee

midnight
minuit
 meenwee

evening soir
 swar

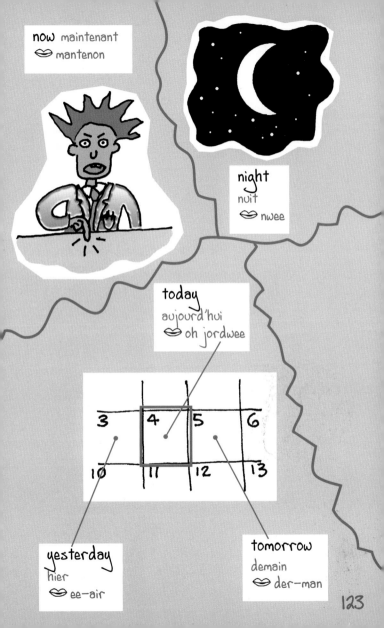

Weather wise

Can we go out?
On peut sortir?
👄 on per sorteer

It's hot
Il fait chaud
👄 eel fay show

It's cold
Il fait froid
👄 eel fay frwa

It's horrible
Il fait mauvais
👄 eel fay movay

It's raining ropes!

In French it doesn't rain "cats and dogs," it rains "ropes!" That's what they say when it's raining really heavily:

Il pleut des cordes
eel pler day kord

124

It's windy
Il fait du vent
👄 eel fay dew von

It's sunny
Il fait du soleil
👄 eel fay dew solay

It's raining
Il pleut
👄 eel pler

It's snowing
Il neige
👄 eel nej

I'm soaked
Je me suis fait tremper
👄 jer muswee fay trompay

It's nice Il fait beau
👄 eel fay bow

Signs of life

taille minimum

minimum height

Eteindre les
téléphones

Turn off your
telephone

Entrée interdite

No Entry

Interdit aux moins
de dix-huit ans

Under 18s not
allowed

Jusqu'à cinq ans
Under 5s only

HORS-SERVICE

OUT OF ORDER

PRIVÉ

PRIVATE